Here to Bump
and
Bump to Hear

By Jane Biehl, PHD

Here to Bump and Bump to Hear: An Assistant Dog's Journey
by Jane Biehl, PhD.

JS Publishers

Contact the author at hearingdog1@gmail.com

Publishers Cataloging In Publication

Here to Bump and Bump to Hear/ Jane Biehl, PhD.

iv, 40 p., |c28 cm.,

ISBN: 978-1-502764-92-8

1. Children's Books. 2. Human-Canine Bond. 3. Service Dogs. I. Biehl,

Jane. II. Title.

636.7002   2012

ACKNOWLEDGEMENTS

No one ever writes or publishes a book alone.
There are so many people who have helped me along the way.

I dedicate this book to my mother, Katherine Biehl, who insisted
I get my hearing dog.

A very special thank you is also extended to Kenzie James, the beautiful
young lady in the photographs.

Cynthia M. Jackson is an extraordinary graphic artist. She put her heart
and soul into the illustrations and photographs of this book and I thank
her so much. She can be reached at Cyndi@paperstrudel.com

Kyla Duffy is the editor of the Happy Tails Books. She is so dedicated and
caring and knowledgeable. She patiently answered my many questions
and guided me along every step of the way. She is a true advocate of the
rescuing of those dogs and cats who need our help so desperately.

I also wish to recognize the volunteers, prisoners, and trainers who give
their precious time to produce caring, helpful companions like Sita.

Sita is my patient and loving companion who has taught me what being
a guardian angel is all about. Thank you Sita!

Sita had been found wandering the streets and was taken to the shelter. She was waiting for a new family to adopt her. Hearing the other caged puppies barking made her scared.

Many people passed Sita's cage. Not one person stopped to play fetch or cuddle. Sita missed her family.

One day a woman stopped in front of Sita. She said, "Your eyes are beautiful. I bet you're a real lover. I see your name is Sita. How would you like to come home with me?"

Sita panted happily.

At her new home, Sita was greeted by four happy dogs and a fat cat. There was plenty of yummy food. Marlys took Sita for long walks and ended each day with a tummy rub.

One day Marlys clipped Sita into her leash. She said, "Sita, you are a special dog and there is a prison where the inmates love dogs and teach them to be assistance dogs. I am taking you there, so you can learn."

Sita was afraid when she entered the prison and saw the bars like the shelter. Some of the men were standing outside of the bars, because they were training the dogs. Marlys led her to one of the men.

"Steve will be your companion. He will teach you commands that will start you on your way to helping people." Marlys handed Sita's leash to Steve.

"Don't worry, Marlys," said Steve. "I'll take good care of her." Sita whimpered when Marlys left. "Hey, girl, it's going to be okay." Steve petted Sita.

Sita loved Steve's gentle hands and decided to trust him. He played with her all day, and Sita slept in a crate next to him at night. Sita learned to sit, stay, and lie down. She enjoyed the treats and pats Steve gave her when she followed his commands.

Several months later, another woman approached Steve and Sita in the cafeteria. Steve knelt down. "Sita, I've taught you all I can. You need to go with Tracy now and learn more commands." Tears welled in his eyes. He handed Tracy the leash.

Sita looked from Steve to Tracy, then back to Steve. She stopped wagging her long tail. "Hi, Sita" said Tracy. I'm your foster mother. You're coming home with me for awhile." Sita whined as Tracy led her out of the prison.

Sita's tail made a big circle when she discovered a whole family of happy dogs and cats at Tracy's house. Tracy also knew how to give her the belly rubs she enjoyed. She got one every night.

Tracy reviewed the commands Sita had learned from Steve. Then she taught her something new. "Sita, I am teaching you to help a deaf person who can't hear important sounds like the doorbell, the telephone or the smoke alarm."

Sita tilted her head as she tried to understand Tracy's words. Tracy gently took Sita's mouth and nose and placed them against Tracy's thigh. "Bump," she commanded. Tracy then knocked on the door and said, "Bump."

At first Sita wanted to bark like the other dogs, but Tracy would gently remind Sita to "bump" her. She repeated the command every time the phone rang. Sometimes Tracy made the smoke alarm sound just so Sita could practice bumping her.

Soon Sita learned that every time she heard a strange noise she needed to bump Tracy. Sita looked forward to the tasty treats she received when she "told" Tracy about the sounds she heard.

One day Tracy placed an orange vest on Sita that said "Do not pet." She explained to Sita that all hearing dogs wear orange vests so people knew what their job is. She told Sita this vest meant she was "getting dressed" and "working."

She said, "Sita, when you are in a vest, you need to stay focused on my commands." In her new vest, Sita could go with Tracy to places the other dogs couldn't. This included restaurants, stores, and offices.

Sita learned not to play with other dogs, sniff around or pick up food off the floor when she wore the vest. When she forgot, Tracy would remind her by a tug on her leash and the word, "no."

At home, Tracy took the vest off and said, "Sita, you can play now."

On Saturdays, Tracy took Sita to Circle Tail, a training center for dogs. Tracy told Sita, "Some of these dogs are assistance dogs. They are learning to help people with disabilities. Other dogs are learning manners."

During training, dogs and their people partners formed a large circle. Some of the dogs pulled wheelchairs, or allowed their people partners to lean on them for balance. Other dogs would retrieve objects like a cell phone for their owners.

In the middle of the circle was a woman giving commands. Sita recognized her as Marlys, the woman who rescued her from the shelter. She panted happily.

Tracy and Sita practiced often at Circle Tail going around the circle, over rails, under tunnels and around barriers. Sita knew how to sit, stay and heel. Tracy would occasionally leave the room where Sita could not see her. She would have to stay until Tracy returned. The two practiced until Sita learned everything she was supposed to know as a hearing dog. Tracy and Sita continued to practice the bumping when she heard sounds at home.

Sita was rewarded by treats and pats on the head. Week after week the two practiced until Sita learned everything she was supposed to know as a hearing dog. Tracy and Sita continued to practice the bumping when she heard sounds at home.

Tracy would take Sita with her out to eat and she learned to sit quietly under the table until she was finished. She would go grocery shopping and walk next to her quietly as they moved through the store. Sita knew she was not permitted to sniff any of the food on the shelves or the floor.

One Saturday, Sita saw a young girl with a pony tail enter the training center. She seemed different from the other children Sita knew. She was frowning instead of smiling.

Tracy led Sita over to the girl. "Sita, this is Jane. She is deaf and needs your help."

Sita put her paw out to shake. Jane's sad eyes lit up. She took the paw. "Hi, Sita. Let's get to know each other."

Sita and Jane practiced going around the circle every Saturday. Sita remembered all the commands she had been taught by Tracy and Steve. For several weeks, Tracy watched Jane and Sita work as a team. Jane would then go home with her parents, and Sita would go back with Tracy and play with the other dogs and cats.

One day, Tracy brought Sita's favorite toy to Circle Tail. After practice, Tracy knelt down. "I've loved having you as a foster dog, but it's time for you to help Jane. You are going to live with her now."

Tracy handed Jane Sita's leash. Sita cried, why was Tracy leaving her? Jane's cell phone rang, and Sita bumped her.

Jane gave Sita a hug. "I need you, girl. I'm so lucky to have you for my ears. I love you, Sita. You're going to live with me and never leave."

Sita licked Jane's face. Somehow she knew Jane wouldn't hand her leash to anyone else again. She would help Jane by being her ears and bumping her. Sita had finally found love and a forever home.

A NOTE FROM THE AUTHOR:

This is a true story except that Sita became my partner when I was an adult, not a child. Sita is a real dog. She was found wandering the streets and taken to a shelter. Marlys rescued her and Tracy was her foster mom. She was trained in two different prisons and a foster home by an organization in Cincinnati, Ohio called Circle Tail.

Sita learned many commands before coming to live with me. We have had a great partnership ever since.

Sita seems to have always known that her job is to look out for me and be my ears. She does her job very well!

I was a therapist for several years and Sita often served as a therapy dog while I worked, licking away the tears of troubled children and adults. Now Sita helps me to teach classes on Deaf Culture and Interpreting at a community college. The students enjoy watching her demonstrate a hearing dog's role. She is a very special dog, and her presence has significantly enhanced my life and the lives of people she meets.

Jane Biehl, PhD, PCC, MLS
Professional Clinical Counselor,
Master's in Library Science

35414905R00025

Made in the USA
Middletown, DE
02 October 2016